Nebraska's Good Ol' Boy Legal System-

In Session

A true story of Lawyer-Judicial Bias in the Civil Court System.

Julie L Carper

ISBN 13: 978-1478365785
ISBN-10: 1478365781

DEDICATION

To my beautiful, wonderful children, whom I will love and cherish for always, written especially for Lea.

Imagine the appeals, dissents and remandments, if lawyers had written 'The Ten Commandments'.
-- Harry Bender

PREFACE

The purpose of the book is written out of frustration with an extremely biased Nebraska court system and how attorneys get away with fraud. It is also meant to create public awareness that the right to be heard is the most difficult, costly procedure in the court system. I have never experienced such a stubborn and obstinate court system who fails to understand issues of due process, refuses to hear issues of attorney misconduct. The court has preferential treatment to attorneys and to those who can afford attorneys.

The biggest obstacle encountered in the Nebraska system is the court refuses to hear serious issues of alcoholism with an attorney, since filing in 2008 the court continually ignored the facts and evidence. They would rather base decisions on drunken hearsay by an attorney than finding of fact. Even refusing to hear issues of alcoholic induced anger incidents of fraud practiced in the court, pulling the evidence and anger induced actions by an attorney. The Court cannot even comprehend the facts that file stamped orders and evidence is missing from the court file and refuses to make an internal investigation as, such documents should be part of the record, state owned documents.

The objective is also to create awareness to the court itself and what people endure with attorney games and legal bull. That if the court simply followed rules and law, none of the incidents would have occurred. The court is responsible for protecting the rights of individuals. What is the purpose of rules and laws if the very court itself does not follow them, or for that matter attorneys who do not follow rules or law. Changes need to be made.

The book merely highlights and exposes serious issues at the federal constitutional level, with attorneys at the state level freely violating rights and take advantage of the trust of the court in biased system. Based a true story within the Nebraska civil court system about a mother's fight for the right to be heard in a biased lawyer-judicial system. Tired of being bullied by a court system who is ignorant of the fact that ex-spouse as an attorney is misusing the legal system to punish.

Truth and justice are not synonymous. Prepare for the fact that attorneys have the privileged right to be heard above all others and they have no problem lying to judges. Nothing worked in the right to be heard in a fair and impartial manner, the book intends to disclose the details and inform the how public practicing attorneys get away with fraud in a preferential court system. The court acted in a manner whereby mean spirited attorneys have more rights than that of a citizen, a woman, a mother, and the court system that bent over backwards to show favor.

Not only is right to be heard is lost but confidence lost in the legal system. In the best interest of the public of legal misconduct and getting the truth heard within the court system simply does not work. If you read blogs, search websites and books, more and more individuals have come forth to speak the truth about a unjust justice system, not in just Nebraska, but nationwide. More and more people are standing up and informing the public as to the courtroom nuances. There are numerous websites giving information as to how attorneys practice and how to fight a biased system, a grassroots trend to fight the judicial indiscretion and injustice. A vast amount of accessible legal information and research than ever before. More and more people are representing themselves as Pro Se based on the distaste for attorneys. It is a growing trend, a trend that courts can no longer ignore.

People are not only educating themselves in the law, many other state courts are providing fill in the blank forms, easy to read rules of the court, both on-line and in clerk's office, assisting with completing the forms and appropriate forms and filing fees. Some states offer courses on rules of the court for pro se representation, and courtesy calls, updates from the judges on motions filed and acknowledged. Other states have very professional civil courts of law, without crass comments of *"so what"* from judges, or stigmatized, prejudicial attitudes in court. Even the federal courts are becoming pro se friendly with easy to read court rules and procedures.

When a person is denied the basic rights of due process, fair and impartial court of law, rights of redress and appeal, your best bet to be heard is not at the state level but at the federal court level, under torts and civil rights. Civil rights are being violated by lawyer-judge bias. An enforceable right or privilege, which if interfered with by the court system itself which has cause great harm and injury.

Julie L Carper

Law students are trained in the case method, and to the lawyer everything in life looks like a case. Edward Packard, Jr.

CONTENTS

ACKNOWLEDGMENTS

To my wonderful and dedicated mother who has been there all the way supportive and communicative whenever needed, morning, noon and night. To my awesome brother and his family for the support and fortitude he has given me. Finally, to my mother-in-law, whom I admire very much and deserves the utmost respect.

Life is about family--- it's not a game!

"Injustice anywhere is a threat to justice everywhere."
- Rev. Martin Luther King, Jr.

When you have no basis for an argument, abuse the plaintiff." -
Cicero

1 GAMING FAMILIES RIGHTS

Win at all costs, give your client the win! That what they pay for! Attorneys know the elements it takes to win a case, often times they work the elements of the win first, inconsistent with ethics or rules. A win for an attorney is ego boosting. The win that hinders the truth, is a game to avoid the truth, you client is going to lose. The concept of just "lie like hell" to win the argument and get the order you want, get the minor children to sign affidavits of who they want to live with and influence them, then see if the other side squirms and let them appeal. But before the appeal attorneys have free access to district court files and can physically pull the evidence of their wrongdoing without letting the higher court know and enforce discipline.

For some attorneys, the "win" is far more important that being civilized and settling matters in a fair and practical mature manner. Some attorneys like theatrics and drama added to the case, it makes great court gossip, it's not just a divorce it's at stage set for making the other parent appear abusive, irrational, or any other abnormal behavior only implement after divorce was filed, otherwise normal prior to filing. Divorce is an action on the stages of the courtroom. Attorneys who play for the staged "win" lack empathy for children and destroy family bonds.

It is all a part of the irresponsible, unethical behaviors by some immature lawyer's. They play it as if the common person is inept and ignorant of law and rules. Exploiting and misusing ethics and rules, the very laws they have an oath to support. Attorneys who play upon the lack of knowledge the common public has on court room rules and law don't' deserve to be attorneys, they are taking advantage of the rights of another and claim ignorance to the court.

Attorneys who practice law as if the common person is naïve, or stupid, have arrogant and ignorant attitudes toward the public themselves, the very public they were sworn to serve. Such attitude reflects poorly on the entire legal profession itself. Attorneys are to be representatives of the public, not self-serving. I have experienced the court system from which attorneys use hearings as a tool to intimidate and humiliate people for the win.

Attorneys need to focus on truth and fairness, settling

matters without legal games, in a civilized manner, thus the meaning of civil court. Establishing truth is should be more important than winning. Laws are written as common sense, out of fairness and implementing due process. Laws were not written to take advantage of rights. Often times the court process misses an element of due process or procedural fairness, but the purpose and intent of the law is to be fair, not play games. Attorneys are sworn by oath prior to becoming attorney that they will uphold the laws of the state and the constitution. They are to preserve and respect the law, ethics and understand rules of the court.

While some attorneys know that the lower courts don't discipline attorneys, leaving them to "lie like hell" for the win and maybe face the consequences later. The buddy system can be lenient. The attorney oath becomes a hypocritical oath. A carte blanche system, with excessive power to attorneys to settle disputes because most judges don't' want to get involved in 'messy' divorce cases.
Yes, there are some lawyers tell the truth and are civil, but it only takes one bad egg to make the entire hen house smell. In this case there are two bad eggs.

Other attorneys treat the business as an assembly line or production of paperwork, they have too much of a case log to focus on one case. The mass production of cases is evident with files lined up in their office along the walls for documents to sign, motions to draft. Production of files are more important than the dealing with people or the very rights they were hired to protect. Dragging me along with the terms "we are going to use the element of surprise," at the meetings. However, in the end, out of disgust with the legal games and a biased judge he wanted to quit, not in civil manner but under stress of the paper work production and with the use of the "F" word in front a eight year old child because he did not want to deal with complicated issues that involved children and opposing an attorney. Quitting on me in the middle of the case was my element of surprise and $12,000 later the only thing he was well practiced was only sticking stamps to the envelopes.

The function of an attorney is to advise his client(s) of the law and to follow that law. They are to conduct themselves in an ethical manner, play by the rules. Any attorney who gives his client advice to lie like hell for the win on the temporary affidavits, delay case progression, knowing that in the end he is going to pull the documents, should not be an attorney. If an attorney's intent is just for the win, regardless of law, they are only in it for status, the name of being an attorney, and not the practice of law, they would not care if their client was lying. Other attorneys will interview as if you are a criminal for filing for divorce, they will even ask if you breast fed your children because the other parent, irate at the situation is now accusing you of horrific family crimes. Other attorneys clearly knew the vendetta scheme it was obvious to the smarter attorneys, the same attorneys who then did not want to get involved. Other attorneys after setting an appointment two weeks prior, made us sit and wait for 45 minutes without acknowledgement or recognition, as if her time was more important and the people who pays her bills with a mirror by her computer screen watching herself talk on the phone.

Then you have status attorneys are there for the win, no matter what, these attorneys have more narcissistic issues than the reality of applying law or considering the effects they have on families. They use the profession simply for notoriety, shaking hands in court as if they have celebrity status, joining several community boards. They utilize the court room as if it were a theatrical stage, a sideshow, creating courtroom drama and a great vocabulary of clichés and distortions of the truth. Status attorneys lack desire to follow the law or adhere to ethics instead use the court as an arena for a contest, a war, between opposing parties. Entertaining themselves in court, willing to do anything for the "win." The objective is in fact wining at all costs it is not about truth, after all it's what their clients pay for.

It is the status attorney, narcissistic for the win, this is willing to even concealing file stamped documents and orders from the district court file just to look good, an impressive win, even to the higher court. By hiding and throwing out his client's evidence of domestic abuse and anger issues associated with alcoholism for the win for his client, pushes boundaries of morality. Status attorneys are willing to even lie to a lower court judge, citing supervised visitation is in a Final Order, when it was not. Status attorneys have no problem lying, misrepresenting fact to even an appellate court judge, knowing that official court documents were pulled from the file. They are the wolf in sheep's clothing; aka judicial brownnoser, succumbing to acting illegally without remorse or respect of laws. They practice law outside the boundaries, offending the dictates of fair play and decency, even common sense.

No honor among thieves. Attorneys who realize other attorneys breach ethics will not turn in each other for violations. It's an honor system, a code of silence, meaning one member does not turn-in or testify against another for violations. Unethical flaws in the judicial system at the expense of another citizens rights. They stick together like glue and when the someone comes into town to investigate matters, they all scatter and have no idea any violations occurred, they have their nose to the grindstone, either way they don't want to get involved, they just want to hear the juicy gossip. They don't want to be exposed for their tricks of the trade, they know more insider tactics than the public need to know. You'd be surprised at what they can get away with in the lower court system. We are at the mercy of the justice system when attorneys and judges band together and have a code of silence, their group, or band of brothers is far more important that the families of the community. Don't let the public know that there is fraud committed in the court system and undermine the public trust.

"Lawyers Are:" The only persons in whom ignorance of the law is not punished.
-- Jeremy Bentham

2 GOOD OL' BOY SYSTEM AT WORK

What makes a good ol' boy system? By definition the good ol' boy system, is a special select group, association; in this case attorneys in the judicial system where bias and favoritism are evident, over and above what is written in rules and law. An attorney's word is considered above all others true and factual, without question of priority and more important than the common citizen.

A good ol' boy system is more interested in protecting attorneys than they are following rules and law. A system where ethics is not a punishable offense in a lower court of law, it has no binding effect, because it's a not a court rule, and ethics is not law. Judge's instead admire the dramatic theatrics by attorneys over basic due process rights. It is a system whereby judges will sign anything to favor an attorney and bend over backwards to break rules and laws to give attorney privilege. The buddy system will also ignore issues of alcoholism and vindictive behaviors by attorneys as if it were common, without reprimand or reversing, or re-thinking their own decisions. All played out as a game or theater in the lower court.

The buddy system ignores how attorneys utilize tricks of the trade, fabricate and a falsify documents without penalty at the lower court level, create phantom evaluations, refuse to pay on an order and refuse visitation without punishment in the lower court. If the common citizen refused to pay on an order, failed to abide by orders, fabricated evidence, they would immediately held in contempt, but not attorneys, the higher court disciplines attorneys, if the matter is appealed. Lower court judges do have limited to no rights to discipline attorneys, thus attorneys have higher privileges the common person does not in a court of law.

The citizen has to a right to appeal the decision with the typical cost of appeal being mid thousand dollar range for a brief and then wait and wait for months to hope for the higher court to punish, reprimand or remand the matter. However, part of the good ol' boy system, is the trusting free access to district court files, whereby they can take out file stamped orders and evidence without any concern from the clerk, Bar Association, county attorney or state attorney general's office. The clerk of the court could care less if the file stamped orders documented in the case were missing from court files. Clerks must not understand the concept of rights of appeal and redress or obstruction of justice. It's not the Clerk's concern of missing file stamped, recorded documents, even though it is part of the job title, to maintain court files.

Even the state attorney general's office is met with the same demeanor, they were fully aware of the missing orders and evidence. The state AG's office is more interested in protecting the buddy judges than the law itself. Their response was "get an attorney." You have public practicing attorneys committing crimes against the state, playing the system, and lying to judges, and the state attorney general's office does seem concerned. The attorney general's office are representatives for the citizens of the state. Why would a state employed attorney make recommendations to pay another absent minded attorney when it is their duty to protect law and citizens? It's a buddy system all the way around.

When judicial complaints are ignored and Bar complaints result in abrasive insults. The bar association is an ineffective means to resolve attorney misconduct in and outside a court of law. Due to the biased buddy system, I have since set up websites, books, flyers, publications and websites to spread the word on the good ol' boy system operating in Nebraska.

The good ol' boy system will even dismiss motions of fraud, domestic abuse and even alcohol induced anger issues of alcoholism filed against attorneys. A good ol' boy system is one that fails to be fair and impartial and gratify an attorney over and above following law and rules. A buddy system that bends over backwards in consideration of and protecting the reputation of an attorney, even with issues of alcoholism, or domestic abuse. Protecting and holding attorneys in esteem over and above protecting the law itself. The last thing a court wants to do create bad press about an attorney, a Mayberry approach to law, where drunk Otis's turn themselves in, to rest in jail for the night, no harm done.

If the word pulled evidence and documents is not emphasized enough within the book, concealing and hiding file stamped and recorded documents is a felony, but the court is not concerned, nor will they investigate.

A good lawyer is a great liar.
--Edward Ward

3 ATTORNEYS BAG OF DIRTY TRICKS

Noted are just a few of dirty tricks experienced within the case that attorneys play especially against Pro Se representation. These same attorneys played the same games even with opposing attorney representation. The purpose is to prove that some attorneys are plain mean, and want to impress only for the win.

<u>Bait and switch affidavits</u>. Prior to temporary hearings taking place, affidavits are to be drafted with the intent to be fair, after all an affidavit is a statement of oath. They are drafted to show best interest and settle matters before the court. Court rules allow each party to view the opposing affidavits, five days prior to submission to court and to address and respond to issues within the affidavits presented. However, attorneys have a dirty trick up their sleeve, they bait and switch out the affidavits the day prior

to the temporary hearing, without the opposing parties knowledge. The affidavits can be switched out without the court realizing the dates or notary date, then changing out wording and replacing them with horrific accusations. The bait and switch affidavit is a surprise element to the opposing party and used to greatly influence judicial decisions in temporary orders. This must be common for attorneys, because another woman recently stated the same happened to her in another district. Judge accepted it.

The same bait and switch can be done with Judge's orders. Often times attorneys are asked to draft orders, the judge will then sign and the attorney records the orders. Orders are not signed or initialed on each page or is there page identification which makes it easy to switch out orders. Case in point, Judge #1 writes a letter citing liberal visitation, however, the citation that the defendant to work in this best mature efforts to allow liberal visitation, the citation was intentionally omitted from the judge's original orders.

Phantom evaluations. Attorneys can provoke a situation whereby there are claims of abuse through a either state agency or dissolution process. Extensive interviews and sessions from an agency could establish the claims of emotional abuse, or other domestic issues. From that agency related interview, and with rights of ex parte

13

communication from the opposing parent, the opposing attorneys can then relay false claims to the court of verifiable incidents of abuse and to subpoena the report from that state agency. An order to seal documents is signed and agreed upon by the court and the documents are faxed directly to the attorney, not the judge as should be or even to the opposing attorney. A sealed document is not privy to the public or opposing parent. In fact with attorneys directly receiving the fax confidential copy can easily be altered. Within the faxed documents are comments from a case worker, not psychologist, that the other parent should be placed under supervised visitation. Drafting an affidavit to the court confirming such message from the case worker solidifies the cause. It's a scheme whereby the other parent has no idea what was stated on the evaluation, or the fact that the other parent did not even participate in any interview process at all. This is called the phantom evaluation. The other parent never was even interviewed but there is a report substantiated by a caseworker of abuse, with recommendations of supervised visitation. But then the denial of the fact that you were interviewed appears as if you are guilty and hiding the fact. While documents were retrieved by an illegal subpoena the faxed document can easily be altered and added to by the use of a fax machine, a machine which can copy as well. Any fax machine can duplicate and add any header you want, it looks official.

Fabricate evidence. With the use of scanners and stamped signatures, technology can "cut and paste" any part of a document to appear official and submitted to the court without question. Scanners can copy colored letterhead and if placed on higher grade paper can be official in appearance. Documents of abuse or irrational behavior, anything can be easily fabricated and presented to the court to influence decisions. The element of surprise for the opposing party. If there is an objection as to the document itself, it makes the opposing party, again, appear guilty, if there are claims that the document is fraud by attorneys, it makes the opposing party have to prove the fact in court or appear unbelievable. Letters from police department or sheriff office of threats, harassment are presented and offered as official evidence. Again, denying the documents and claiming fraud against attorneys gives you the appearance of an unstable parent.

Fail to mail motions to opposing side. Attorneys will send out motions and petitions without knowledge the opposing party, even though service was certified. Filing petitions and motions to the court and never receiving a copy demonstrate opposing side as unorganized, sloppy in their response and lack of knowledge of what the document states. Being Pro Se is especially tough because attorneys have full access to electronic document filing, easily referencing recent filings. Not giving adequate notice, especially to a Pro Se is used to offset rights of redress and response. Any upset to an attorney by Pro Se representation affects an attorneys ego and reputation among other small town attorneys. They become the "gossip of the chamber" if upset by a Pro Se.

Provoke and create police incidents. A known tactic is to call police to create incidents. Simply by calling 911 and fabricating stories of harm, concern, or verbal threats creates a police intervention and generates a police report. The day after the incident, call your attorney, mislead them in the facts of a police incident and obtain the report. It's easy to give your attorney and the court the intended wrong impression of the opposing spouse. The attorney will then call the judge and relay that same message of urgency, something needs to be done, it is all the intent of that attorney to create impact. Easily done. Continue this action at least once a month to give the court a false impression of behavioral patterns. Establishing a pattern of police/sheriff reports to court of calls against the opposing side will easily create the wrong effect and punitive orders.

Delay Case Progression. Contrary to court rules,

dragging out a dissolution matter can easily be excused based on abuse, neglect, allegations of finding of fault. Dragging out the case is costly, attorney's fees can skyrocket, sucking out your life savings and earnings. Financially, and emotionally draining the other parent into giving up the fight, it will become a losing battle. Know your district court rules, even prior to filing, and even if you have an attorney, that attorney is not going to automatically advise you of law or enforce anything until you tell him.

Know the laws, as well, if you don't that attorney may walk all over your rights, his case load maybe phenomenally high and overwhelming and he has no interest in fighting the law unless he receives direction.

<u>Obstruction of Justice</u>. Attorneys have influence to obstructing rights of appeal and redress. The court system fails to implement the Federal Rules of Civil Procedure, or other policies which can track and number orders, pleadings, evidence submissions, motions, even initial pagination within pleading. Physical files are separately maintain from the electronic filings, physical files contain sensitive information of affidavits, and is not publically shared. However, with free attorney access to District court files, knowing that there is an inadequate means as to track state owned documents once they are file stamped

and recorded by the court, become a game to some attorneys. Free records access by attorneys is allowed under court rules supplied by the higher court. Withholding evidence and file stamped orders, however are not allowed but there is nothing to track the system and challenge missing documents. Without hesitation it is tactic that experienced attorneys play upon novice attorneys and pro se representation and the courts. Apparently the clerks of the court don't place a system of file contents only until after a praecipe is processed for appeal. Attorneys can replace evidence with other evidence, pull file stamped order and acknowledged evidence from a file without the clerk or the court reporters knowledge. Some court reporters work part time and the clerk is to maintain the contents of the file. Attorneys have free reign to go inside a district clerk's office, filing system and court files.

Obstruction of Justice under the terms of Bill of exceptions. By definition a bill of exception is a legal pleading filed to complain on appeal about a matter that would not otherwise appear in the record, however, since previous file stamped orders, and evidence acknowledged by the court and are of record, the appellate court denied fraud and ruled res judicata under the requirements of a bill of exceptions. No particular form of words is required in a bill of exception. But the objection to the court's ruling or action, and the ruling complained of, must be stated with sufficient specificity to make the trial court aware of the complaint. The bill of exceptions was irrelevant in the matter because previous orders and pleadings were wrongly influenced judicial decisions and orders and evidence were already part of the record. It is apparent that attorneys can easily confuse the higher court with such concepts, knowing that they physically pulled file stamped orders. . The appellate court is adamant that a verbatim record is required for appeal, if a two day hearing costs, was set up by attorneys, and was nothing but a waste of time and continued lies, how do you fight this Simply because a bill of exceptions was not provided, the basic rights to assets, children, and other constitutional rights should not be denied. A bill of exceptions should neither affirm the matter in favor of the opposing party, or federally protected rights to due process, children and assets. It's a verbatim record of insubstantial meaning.

Take advantage of Clerk's inadequacies. In many other states, the clerk of the court is autonomous from attorney influence. In fact clerks are behind glass windows, and attorneys have to stand in line just as other common civilians to file motions and pleadings. Attorneys in other states do not have free access to district court files. Clerks of the courts in many states have forms for pro se representation and know the rules of the court without attorneys yelling in the background to confuse the clerks of citing rules, rather attorney tell clerks any reference of rules to a Pro Se is practicing law.

Lie and Deny. Any complaint to the Bar Association is dealt with a "lie and deny" claim. It is a common canned phrase an attorney might state "the judge did not consider this or did not rule on these documents." Bar complaints don't work, especially if the buddy judge rules in their favor, the Association will ignore the possibility of bias in the court. Evidence can be presented as complaints to the Bar, but they are not going to analyze any documents, thus their conclusion does not leave much for consideration, nor would they care if a judge based decisions without evidence, simply on hearsay. Even the Bar Association holds the common person of regard as being stupid. Motions of fraud are brought up as the same defense, "your honor, my client wouldn't lie [he's an attorney]." It's a game easily played by attorneys who are good at two-facing the court and the bar association.

Starve out the other guy. Attorneys can use punitive orders, fabricated evidence, prolonging the case progression and adding up costs of representation and then failing to pay on an order, all to starve out the other guy. Starving them out of everything emotionally possible. Deny them rights of visitation, but make sure your attorney client gets the maximum amount of child support based on income potential, even while unemployed, the monies can be taken out of the bank account.

Ambush guardians and psychologists. Under court rules any guardian that is to be appointed should be within a month of custody, otherwise I would not recommend obtaining a motion to seek a guardian at any time. In our case, after months of false affidavits and being denied the rights to any reasonable visitation based on an attorneys "word" a guardian was appointed, nine months after custody was granted. By that time any vindictive custodial parent would have already gotten to the children in convincing them of the other "bad" parent. Ambushing them with numerous false statements, fabricated documents and knowledge of law, to sway decisions.

Guardians base decisions solely on hearsay, they do not require anyone to take an oath as to what they are stating as true and factual. In other words the controlling parent, alcoholic parent, or narcissistic, sociopathic parent will exaggerate like hell, produce fabricated documents and punitive orders (contrary to law) to prove their point. It's not the job of the guardian or psychologist to verify the documents for fraud and none of the documents are presented in court. Only the determination of the guardian or psychologist is presented. Thus appointed guardians don't work.

Psychologists are in the same boat, they don't swear any one in as to telling the truth and will accept any document that comes there way, they are not obligated to see if the documents or statements are true or factual. In this case, a fabricated sheriff's report was given to the psychologists, unknowing of the fact that a sheriff's office does not make reports of other people, especially people they have never met, a phantom report with a fictitious cell phone number of a sheriff, which is actually a personal friend impersonating a sheriff. It is all a set up attorneys know how to play the system.

Ex Parte Communication. Another trick, call your lawyer, make numerous false statements to wrongly impress the court system, get Ex Parte Orders, that will surprise the heck out of the opposing party, out of shock and dismay from what the intent was by the Orders. Even for minor items, such as contempt for dogs, and in another case contempt threats from a judge with ex parte orders of where children should go to school. The court meddles way too much in the personal business of families and without being in the best interest of families, creating more trauma to families because of their adversarial style of dominating control in a dissolution matter. Judges think they know more about your family than you do and will make decisions irrelevant to parental preferences. Ex Parte Orders intend to exclude, and eliminate the opposing party from any just resolve in issues. If two parties cannot resolve issues first and foremost the court still has no right to interject and order people in personal family matters. Personal parental issues should not be the state's prerogative to dictate and interfere. I don't see a court interjecting in married people's lives so why would they interject with a dissolution matter as if once you file divorce loose parental consideration rights are lost. Because it is a biased system.

"Lawyers Are:" Those who earn a living by the sweat of their brow-beating. -- James G. Huneker

4 THE SET UP

Contemplating divorce it probably the most emotionally stressing situation anyone can go through. It is common for dissolution matters to become abrasive, it's not the parent, but the attorneys who become even more vindictive adding courtroom drama and taking advantage of court privileges, all to create animosity and unequal division. My fault lies in the fact that the spouse is an attorney.

Dissolution was filed September 2008 myself, as the plaintiff with Temporary Hearing set October 31, 2008. The defendant, as an attorney, with knowledge of law and out of retaliation, set up affidavits with intent to find fault, through a convincing plot of Plaintiff being unstable parent by manipulating the bait and switched affidavits and documents centered around an out of control, false mental condition. This shows that attorneys will go to the extreme to make up and exaggerate stories for the win. They intentionally switched the affidavits to wrongly influence judicial decisions. This is part of the drama some immature attorneys utilize, or some people misrepresent to their attorneys to create an over-reaction to the court motions.   Any sort of change often scares people, especially attorneys, because any change may affect their pocketbook and reputation.

In this case, the court allowed to grant leave for hearings, and allowed affidavit based orders, it was an intentional set-up by the defendant and his counsel. Granting leave for hearing is egregious violations of due process inconsistent with an individual's rights. Granting leave of hearing also denies rights to respond to affidavits or view affidavits prior to the deadline of submission to court.   Affidavit only orders denies full rights of hearing and due process, the sworn statements of oath basically took away rights without hearing and right to respond, yet the court must have believed that general public is stupid at rights of due process.   Violations of due process, absent of fact and ignorance of binding legal issues of the case is all a part of the buddy legal system.

The kicker of the deal was that the defendant and his counsel, as attorneys under oath of their office, revised the primary affidavit, the day before the temporary hearing, October 30, 2008. Revised without notice or knowledge by the court or responding party. The defendant's affidavit contained various false, slanderous statements with the intent to harm and win custody and set exclusion from the home almost immediately.

As a result, in November 2008, an Order to Exclude, Ex Parte Orders were made with less than twenty days for Plaintiff as a mother, to move out of the home, loss of property rights, prior to settlement, without hearing, showing of cause to do so as required by law. The court championed the defendant as an attorney, requiring no evidence or need for plaintiff for hearing; excluded from my own home, without following any course of law.

Custody was based on minor children signing affidavits with the phrase, mom is going to be kicked out of the home, I want to live with my dad. Such statements are coercion rather than a showing of parental responsibility. Custody was granted to a man who for ten years made child support payments because he could not make a parental commitment, he wanted to be free and single. The same parent who had pervious court ordered anger management, and protection order from issues of alcoholism and domestic abuse, becomes custodial parent. Not only did misspell the all children's names incorrectly on his affidavit; he didn't even know how to operate a mop or cook spaghetti, but the court named the attorney the custodial parent, based on the bait and switch affidavit. The good ol' boy system.

As plaintiff, unknowing of rules and laws at the time of filing dissolution, never understood why the court agreed to grant leave and submit affidavits, until an emerging pattern of fraud, affidavits made in bad faith, slander, character assassination tactics intentionally made to wrongfully influence judicial decisions, set to make the other parent look inferior, in my case, incompetent. Both the court and my attorney, believed statements made by an attorney were true and factual and would not risk his practice of law to present such statements. The first affidavit referenced the wording "she failed to inform her doctor." I had no idea what he meant, until one year later, it was finally, finally disclosed that my ex-husband as an attorney swore to the court I was treated and diagnosed with mental disorder. Gee, no one told me that I was treated and diagnosed by my spouse, or anyone for that matter. Under ex parte communication privilege he relayed the hugely, false information to the court. It was all a set-up.

From November 2008 to May 2009, contrary to due process and contrary to rules of case progression, they played stall tactics, so legal costs of representation became unaffordable. It was all a set up. Affidavits submitted by the defendant were nothing but verbal attacks utilized to complicate issues and confuse the court. As an attorney he continually fought any decent rights of visitation without evidence or showing of cause, his drunken hearsay. Simply because he was an attorney, court granted him favor. None of the documents or statements presented by defendant can be verified or certified as original and genuine by the source of the entities.

Both Attorneys, in their win-it-all cause, abused the context of the law and set up false claims to find ways to influence judicial decisions by fabricating documents and a continual barrage of false statements. A prime example is a statement of supervised visitation from caseworker, contrary to state policy and law. Under law caseworkers are not psychologists and can never make such recommendations without interviewing both parties and an extensive process following the exact course of law as set forth by statute and policies. The sealed document was merely "faxed" document from which the original can not be produced in it's exact form as presented to the court. The altered document and sealed under protective order to the judge in March 2009, set to mislead and wrongly influence the court. Prior to appeal and against the recommendations of the judge, the sealed document was removed by the attorneys to prevent discovery of fraud at the appellate court level and then filed a motion to recuse the judge.

Numerous false documents and fabricated statements were made by the defendant and his counsel during the course of the matter from November 2008 to December 2009, leading up to the final hearing, all to wrongly influence judicial decisions. However, prior to appeal more than 300 pages of documents as acknowledged in the orders and the file stamped orders become missing from the district court file. Since orders were affidavit based, no record of hearing since there were no hearings, and orders acknowledged evidence for the purposes of the order, there was no need for a bill of exceptions. Even under current court rules and various laws, orders and affidavits are part of the record and should be within the court file. However, they are missing from the appellate court file in 2010.

At this point, after orders of exclusion, supervised visitation, even though they were made contrary to any evidence, contrary to law, no other attorney would get involved after seeing an order to exclude and order of supervised visitation. All based on drunken hearsay by attorney. However, if this is how attorneys behave, who needs them? What's the purpose of an attorney if he can not stand up to his own professional oath. It was their intention to leave a mother hanging on with no rights of redress or rights to be heard.

A gunfight at the OK Corral would have been quicker, less dramatic with only a brief moment of pain. Based on the extreme bias judges have for attorneys, I can understand why the Nebraska court system implemented some cheap metal detectors by the courtrooms. Metal detectors in the civil court are the first indication of biased judge.

When you are up against a biased judicial system and vindictive attorney's no one can go the distance inside the nasty arena of the court. Be proactive, get a website, make contacts, send out flyers, copy email addresses of all the attorneys in the state bar association and send out emails of the buddy system; send mailers to the community of the misbehaviors of attorneys and how the court fails to be fair and impartial. Do everything you can, because the court system continually fails in the right to be heard. Go outside the state court system.

I'll never discuss my lawyer's character in his absence, so let's discuss his absence of character!   --Michael Lara

5 FRAUD PRACTICED WITHOUT HESITATION

It all seems too easy under a lenient court system to have attorneys make numerous material misrepresentations to the court, lie to judges, fabricate evidence, take advantage of judicial trust and then physically pull file stamped and recorded documents from the court file without hesitation. How did this happen?

Nebraska court system is one of the last remaining states to implement the Federal Rules of Civil Procedure, and in fact it is the last state that argues in evidence and requires a bill of exceptions as part of the of the record to determine if argument was made by motions as to the introduction of evidence and the denial of evidence. Most states accept all evidence into a hearing without argument prior to submission.   Acceptance of evidence without argument relieves the judge from bias and allows him to rule on the evidence as they see fit. The Nebraska civil court system also has an archaic system in tracking orders and evidence. The court will never know what orders and evidence are missing from the district court and appellate court file because they never continually track documents simultaneously together. File submission to the appellate court is done with the physical paper file and the clerk only tracks documents only after a notice of appeal is filed. There is an inadequate tracking system because no audits are made between the electronically filed documents or paper tracking system as pleadings, and motions are filed in at the moment. In between that time the physical file remains unlogged only until there is an appeal. While many court systems, number and track the orders, evidence and even initial page numbers within file stamped documents, the Nebraska Civil Court system does not. Thus fraud, concealment of fact and removal of file stamped orders, evidence, tracking the motions because easy for attorneys.

Most states have already implemented the Federal Rules as a level playing ground for all those involved, saving time as argument for evidence. Arguing evidence to before it is to introduced, and not allowing the judge to view the evidence easily creates appearance of judicial bias. Some slime-ball attorneys argue every piece of evidence in a hearing to waste court time, and they have 1,001 ways to dismiss evidence; "*my client is unfamiliar with the evidence, it's fraudulent, it's been digitally altered; it's not a true representation of fact; there is conflicting evidence; the judge has already made his decision from a previous order, your honor my client would never lie, he's an attorney."* In Nebraska the failure to implement the Federal Rules has become a game of arguing evidence for the judge to consider and argument on the facts, such waste of time in arguments, easily reverts to fraud due to the free access of the district court files thereafter if an appeal is made.

As Plaintiff, discovery of the missing file stamped documents were made after opposing counsel filed a motion to Summary Affirm the matter at the appellate level. Summary Affirm based on case law, as if I had failed to introduce the documents in as evidence at hearing. You don't introduce previously file stamped recorded orders and evidence already acknowledged in the orders, at a another hearing, orders which end up missing from the appellate court file. Case was then argued under the terms of res judicata. Of course the appellate court bought it, because they cannot even open up a previous appellate case file and reference the fact that there are missing file stamped orders and evidence acknowledged within the orders. The appellate court cannot comprehend a brief specifically outlining which orders and evidence that is missing, and cant get up off their chairs to look at a previous file, or call a judge in the lower court to see how the case was handled. Res judicata would only apply if there was a complete submission of court files in the matter. Hiding file stamped orders and evidence previously acknowledged in the orders restricted the appeal process. But the court again is bias and fails to hear both sides equally, or comprehend how fraud is practiced in the court system. A very complacent system of justice.

Since the file submission was incomplete, res judicata was restricted because the same court file from the lower court did not travel up to the appellate court. Collateral attacks were made to the fact that original orders were obtained by fraud and then fraudulent information was removed prior to appeal. The limited exceptions to res judicata would apply, because the original judgment even outside the appeals, was based on procedural issues. Not based on the wisdom of the earlier court's decision because of the removal of evidence illustrating an attorneys behaviors with alcoholism. The court is merely basing decisions on previous lawyer-judge bias without proper review.

The Appellate Court assumed the attorney was correct in his filing and did not even read the brief or review the evidence, or lack of evidence to support the final order.

The good ol' buddy system Summary Affirmed, an

administrative review, without the requirement of the opposing counsel's brief, unknowing file stamped orders and evidence was missing from the file.

Summary affirmed without reviewing the case file or any brief and an incomplete file.

Summary affirmed based on the failure to submit an (irrelevant) bill of exceptions, whereby the court then denies any rights of children and assets simply by the failure to submit the verbatim record. Due process rights continually denied.

Summary affirmed fraud, affidavits made in bad faith, exclusion contrary to law and lack of due process, how convenient the system is for attorneys.

After a notice if discovery of missing documents were sent to the opposing attorneys, and without an attorney myself, out of panic these attorneys misused the fabricated sealed document, or phantom evaluation under a new judge, #2. The panic stricken attorneys misrepresented fact stating that an Order had been handed down of supervised visitation. An order that was modified out of jurisdiction. They typed up an order and claimed supervised visitation was agency related without noting supervisory entity within the order, as required by law, thirty days incarceration and misdemeanor charge for failure to take parenting class, all contrary to rules and law, there was not even discussion at the hearing to support any of the order.

Both supervised visitation and incarceration was a set up as a deterrent for their misbehaviors. After discovery was made and informed them of the missing documents he was then heavily drinking, 10 hours at the bar, as witnessed by another attorney. Out of concern for my youngest, I kept her. They then relayed to the new judge I was under supervised visitation as in the final order. It was a set to prevent discovery of the missing documents, it was an order stating don't' come and visit your children not only will you be in jail, you will have limited visitation rights and supervised. Yes thirty days jail time for a parenting class. I have seen people with DUI charges, hit and run charges get out of jail 28 days sooner than with a violation of a parenting class. This is the Nebraska court system. There is even public record of a bar owner who had a three violations in one night, leaving the scene of an accident, hit and run and driving while intoxicated serving only a four day sentence. Inappropriate alcoholic behaviors must be the accepted norm, the buddy system will help. In Nebraska, it's not what you know, but who you know.

These attorneys continually misused the fabricated sealed document, or phantom evaluation. It was misused as a complete misrepresentation of fact to "go away" and not have any rights of redress or visitation and then telling Judge #2 it was in the final order. Continually denied the right to be heard to the fraudulent claims, the court never once listened. Appealing the supervised visitation order would be pointless because the opposing side would file a motion to dismiss, citing supervised visitation is agency related, in the juvenile court jurisdiction. It's all a ruthless, mean game played by attorneys.

The court file contains no court substantiated documentation, motion, petition, even discussion, either agency or non-agency related to enforce supervised visitation, but the judge bought their lies and signed the order. The September 2010 Order made without following exact course of law, written without notation of supervisory entity as required by law. I never knew where to go for supervised visits, with no rights of visitation for more than (11) eleven months. It was all an ill-mannered, misrepresentation of fact by opposing attorneys to offset rights of redress and prevent discovery of their own wrongdoing. Finding attorney representation in the matter was intentionally difficult, Anytime I would call an attorney, all they would have to state is supervised visitation, and deprive rights of decent representation.

Even the Final Order does not comply with law or rules due to conduct constituting fraud. defendant, as an attorney, breached oath of office and took advantage of attorney privilege, to mislead the court to find legal ways to take away rights. Actions included exclusion from the home, loss of custody, a stay at home mother, no vested rights to assets, savings or home equity. Due to legal harassment and bullying tactics, I moved out of state for monetary and security issues; still denied any rights to be heard, an attorneys word is preferential.

Based on solely on hearsay and abuse of discretion through fraud, orders were made contrary to law, without evidentiary support, or showing of cause. Court now has stigmatized me as a plaintiff basing the adverse judgments and orders as an indication of character. Yet the orders have no evidentiary support to back them. All of it resulted in a denial of rights to equity or fair hearing. This was the intent of the attorneys. The court continually favored the defendant, as an attorney, failing to acknowledge dynamics of alcoholism, basing decisions from his excessive verbal attacks. Since the case was improperly Summary Affirmed in 2010, current Judge #3, refuses to modify the Final Order, even with knowledge plaintiff has moved out of state with no rights of adequate visitation. These attorneys, are very unprofessional, they deny rights of redress, by pulling file stamped documents, get the matter Summary Affirmed. concealing evidence and file stamped orders would verify that no genuine issue of material fact exists and then dangle the Affirmation to the judge stating you can't doing anything, not even modify the order, abide by the appellate court's order, judge!

"Lawyers Are:" Those who lie, conceal and distort everything and slander everybody.
-- Jean Giraudoux

6 TRASH TALK OR FACT

Apparently the court system cannot distinguish fact from trash talk by an attorney, because they continually ruled in the attorneys favor. Verbal assaults and slander wins over fact and reason, in a Nebraska court of law, it's how this case was won. While slander and misrepresentations of facts to influence judicial decisions, is a civil rights violation with the intent to bring harm to another person's reputation, the court does not care. Various pleadings and motions were filed by the directly by the defendant as an attorney. These pleadings contained nothing more than slanderous words, verbal insults, degrading comments, and should not be allowed. The court cannot distinguish verbal abuse and insults from fact within legal writings, nor do they care.

Courts are to set standards from which pleadings and motions should be accepted or that they should contain fact, not baseless insults and frivolous claims and attorneys are to redact irrelevant statements within the pleadings or affidavits. Offensive language in a pleading or motion is unprofessional, it's a form of public disrespect of the party and the court, yet the court does not enforce rules of redaction.

Since an attorneys word is held over and above the rights of all others, without the requirement for evidence the court accepts the put-downs, and verbal abuse and ruled in his favor, inconsiderate of fact. Wording within the pleadings included recommendations of being institutionalized, psychotic, and ignorant, such discourteous, untrue statements are typical alcoholic debilitating deficit traits. It is difficult to tell if judges even read pleadings, if it's signed by an attorney who representing an attorney the judge considers trash talk as truthful and of fact.

Neither attorney is reprimanded for filing pleadings containing false, slanderous statements, because it's a buddy system. Is the purpose of a court of law to insult and degrade, intimidate and humiliate citizens? No. But then again, attorneys have a higher priority of the right to be heard than the general public, even those as defendants. Never once did the court listen as to issues of alcoholism and verbally abusive traits associated with the disease by an attorney. The truth is that lower courts don't discipline attorneys, enforce rules and law. When the lower courts fail to discipline attorneys, it is a way of protecting and encouraging misconduct.

Even the State Bar Association uses insulting tactics when initiating concern over issues of alcoholism. Cliché's' such as "your just bitter because you lost," in April 2012 I was told by a state bar employee that I need psychological help because I lost custody and to give it up. Apparently the use of rude, cheap shots is common in the legal profession. It is a way to offend, publically insult, to stop a complaint, or disrupt conversation. The trash talk does nothing but create animosity, and continued incivility by attorneys, they are inconsiderate behaviors; used by publically licensed buttheads. The offenses deter the opposing party from responding, or preventing a dignified answer to the court and instant wrong impression without reprimand. It's a shut-up, don't bother me- go away tactic.

Both attorneys and the Bar association are not to be the vulgar mud-slingers, they are to act in a truthful and professional manner, at least that is what is understood under the rules of ethics. Representative of a higher professional standard does not mean to degrade and insult people. Professionals who are to resolve issues in a courteous manner, not file frivolous pleading, act out in dramatic outrageous conduct or make slanderous statements. It is obvious that the legal profession approves of staged courtroom drama and scandal, otherwise they would have never played this game. Maybe dramatic incidences are used to grab the attention of the judge, or that alcoholic's love drama as well, as a focus on the other person, court's succumb to anger traits faster than the boring truth. This type of fictional court drama and slander is better than judge's chamber gossip or reality television.

I don't think you can make a lawyer honest by an act of legislature. You've got to work on his conscience. And his lack of conscience is what makes him a lawyer.   --- Will Rogers

7 ISSUES OF ALCOHOLISM AMONG ATTORNEYS

It is noted that the legal profession highest prevalence of alcohol abuse and depression related to stress than any other profession. Often times alcoholism goes unnoticed until extreme behaviors become apparent. It's a hidden disease. There are some studies from various state bar associations which claim that one out of three lawyers suffer from alcoholism. Alcoholism has varying stages according to a variety of articles and websites, it is a disease that the court system should not ignore, especially among attorneys. When a legal system ignores or overlooks the serious issues of the disease they can do irreparable harm. An alcoholic does not know normal, nor should a court should choose alcoholic drama over fact, civility and cooperation. This is exactly how the court ruled, by the high alcoholic drama.

Only through education and AA counseling can a person learn to recognize the traits and symptoms, how to react and understand the nature of the disease. Like myself, only until a person is out of the situation and understand the patterns and behaviors become evident. Even going through the steps program you can learn how and why they become alcoholics. Alcoholic patterns and behavior traits by an attorney which can easily be established in court of law, but continually denied. The court failed to recognize the source of the verbal assaults and fabricated documents, statements of oath were originated by the traits of alcoholism. Instead, the court, believed the attorney simply because he was an attorney and would not lie.

An attorney with alcoholism can easily utilize the punch words from previous cases knowing what judges are offended by under their use of alcoholic reasoning. Alcoholics are very convincing and will fabricate, exaggerate, place blame, anything to justify their behaviors. Alcoholics don't know the concept of normal; chemical reactions in the brain tend to go on extreme highs and lows and overreact to stressful situations. They see no wrong in their actions or words for it is a way of protecting their lifestyle and what has meaning to them. In this case, fraud, or deceit to the court, alcohol induced anger traits.

Previously submitted evidence, testimony can establish a pattern and history of the debilitating deficits in judgment making and problem solving, however the court completely ignored the issues. What makes it worse is that his fellow attorney, with knowledge of his client's unacceptable behaviors, interceded and denied the submission of court documents prior to appeal to conceal such fact to the higher court. It was done not only to distort and hide the truth at the appellate level, but to preventing discovery of a "cunning baffling and wicked" disease. That is not justice.

Since the evidence and orders were physically pulled, and concealed yet the court continues to base decisions solely on the trust of attorneys. The court assumed that allegations and evidence presented by me as the Plaintiff was irrelevant, as a way of getting back.

Based on the evidence presented to the court, preferential treatment for an attorney is obvious, the system believes that the parent with vindictive traits, associated with alcoholism, is the better parent, simply because he is an attorney. Nor can the court system be so uneducated in addictive traits and deal with the public on a continual basis they fail to recognize the dynamics and alcohol induced anger traits.

The court ruled to accommodate an attorney simply because an attorney should not lie. By ignoring the real issues and indulging an attorney, they actually encouraged bad behaviors from serious, deadly disease. The system has a way of protecting attorneys.

It does not matter even if an attorney is an alcoholic, the fact remains that if an attorney cannot use cognitive rationalized reasoning for his actions, and disregard law and rules to commit serious legal offenses against the state during the course of business, they should be punished just as any other common citizen is punished. Attorneys are not above the law. Nor should a court ever base decisions simply drunken hearsay or succumb to anger statements from an attorney to appease him. The court simply fails to understand what it is like to live with an alcoholic and the confusion, degradation, and depression associated with the disease.

"Lawyers Are:" People whose profession it is to disguise matters. -- Thomas More

8 CAUSE AND EFFECT

When orders are made contrary to law without any due process or rights to hearing, it affects the outcome and gives others the right to take advantage of unfair gain. The order to exclude made in November 2008 without hearing with less than twenty (20) days to vacate my own deeded property. This exclusion order gave the defendant an opportunity to tell the children I lied to the judge and was kicked out. It gave him the right to control every aspect of property rights and denial of those rights. It also gave him the right to control every aspect of visitation rights and the denial of those parental rights. The same effect occurred with a false statement of supervised visitation from the phantom evaluation, confusion set in, giving the children again the wrong impression, telling the children to stay away from the mother. Denial of any visitation rights, loss of bonds with children, improper orders and enforcement of orders based on deceit does more harm to a family the courts will never understand the damage to relationships. Naturally, children begin to doubt the other parent and become prone to vulnerable parental attacks by the controlling, domineering parent.

When a parent is placed on supervised visitation from an order made in September 2010 without any supporting evidence, or following any course of law, without any rights of visitation or bonding, such actions by attorneys is done with malice and intent to ruin relationships. The order of supervised visitation was made out of jurisdiction and without noting supervisory entity, I had no rights of seeing children for more than eleven months. This ruins bonds with children. Does the court care, or ensure visitation, no. Judge #2 completely ignored phone calls and pleadings asking where to go for visitation, why it was enforced, there is no evidence. I was completely ignored as to rights of visitation. This is worse than vindictive it is cold and callous acts by attorneys, who have no respect for law or family.

An order of supervised visitation without following any course of law is proof judges will sign anything to favor an attorney. Such an order is nothing less than insensitive and callous and ignorant of the law themselves. This legal matter has gone on for more than three vindictive years, and when a person is bullied and pushed around by the courts to service an attorney without following any course of law, people get fed up with the system. None of this would have ever happened if the court was fair and impartial, followed law, and did not give excessive attorney privileges.

Courts are senseless when it comes to rights of children, and parents, issues of domestic abuse and alcoholism. <u>I am divorcing my spouse not my children, and until there is significant due process, evidence and proper course of law, the court has no right to interfere in anyone's parental rights.</u>

The judicial benches are dominated by males, who fail to understand the sacrifices women make to parenting, and maintaining the household. Sacrifices to careers and education were made, even as a single parent.

Showing concern for my children from the effects of alcoholism was sought after with contempt by the opposing party. Contempt, as if I had no right to protect children from the detriments of his anger issues. The worst thing possible is to give custody and rights to a vindictive parent, the spite is directed toward the other parent in all avenues even the children. To which evidence presented in the case of verbal abuse, physical abuse, emotional and financial abuse, is a mere extension of legal and domestic abuse, by attorneys, nonetheless.

When Judge #3 states they are just playing a game, is no excuse, it's protecting bad behaviors at the other parent's expense. No judge should ever make such statement. Judges are to control the misbehaviors of attorneys, however they are hesitant and end up protecting and encouraging such bad behaviors because there are no real consequences at the lower court level.

The same vindictive behaviors continue from the custodial parent. In May 2012 sent notice to the custodial parent of rights of summer visitation, and ignored for three weeks. Sent court a notice of fact and then set a place and date for exchange with the words directly from the judge that the sheriff can be called if he fails to appear. Low and behold he fails to appear, he's an attorney.

When I can not get visitation rights to see my child, the judge's word meant nothing, the order means nothing, because attorneys do not have to abide by law or orders. Two weeks later I receive a letter from his counsel with two different excuses why an attorney failed to abide by an order and show, citing a no show on my behalf and unpaid bond to which he did not want the daughter to be exposed to seeing a parent placed in jail. This is always their intent, to threaten and to intimidate, attorneys none the less.

Both two-faced answers by attorneys were inexcusable and inappropriate, they are always justifying lies with stupid answers and the court buys it. The bond is paid on a false contempt and paid time stamped receipts prove we were in at that exact location as stated. It's a game and since he's an attorney, no big deal. He has all rights to justify his behaviors at any time. Relationships are growing distant but does the court care- no! This is a typical alcoholic making excuses and then making up bizarre lies to justify bad behavior. It does not matter what pleadings are filed by a pro-se they will never be heard, contempt, nothing. It's a good ol' boy system with no right to be heard, not unless you're an attorney or have an attorney, which will cost you a fortune. It's all a game at a child's expense, irreparable damage to a family. This is law?

The court did nothing but embarrass me out of my rights, in front of my community, neighbors, friends and most of to my family, by failing to follow law, and bending over backwards to break rules and law to favor an attorney, and alcohol induced anger.

The trial lawyer does what Socrates was executed for: making the worse argument appear the stronger. -- Judge Irving Kaufman

9 SELF-GOVERNING, SELF-SERVING SYSTEM

The legal system is a self-governing, it controls the power to discipline and sanction those within the profession. The Nebraska court system, lower court and higher court refuse to hear issues of bias and internal issues of fraud or attorney misconduct in the matter. The court system is autonomous within any other checks and balances in the other branches of government.

The court system is also self- serving system especially if you're an attorney. The benefits of being an attorney and getting the orders to their own interest, without the concern for others rights or law. Self-serving to the fact that the court bent over backwards to appease attorneys, contrary to rules and law. The court is not strict with rules or laws when it comes to attorneys, they let them play the game without any regard for the other person on the receiving end of their games. The lower court did not care about the truth, nor about procedures.

Not only do some attorneys play upon that judicial bias and favoritism to influence judges, they game the judges who entrust them to be honest and forthright. Some attorneys will lie to get what they want from the orders. Attorneys know that it is the higher court who reprimands, sanctions and disciplines, and they have many ways of avoiding discovery of their wrongdoing, by disallowing file stamped and recorded documents from being reviewed by the appellate and district court. Many Nebraska attorneys have free access to district court records, they are able to conceal file stamped orders and evidence from the district court files prior to appeal. As a result, missing documents and orders, not only interferes with one's rights of appeal and redress, it gets the orders you want without a chance to modify, and prevents discovery of illegal attorney activities to higher court.

As proof the system is self-serving: When an attorney says I want to kick out my spouse, the court does so without any course of law;. when the attorneys says he wants custody because of a false claim of a mental illness, the court says sure, we don't' need to see the woman, we believe you; when an attorney says limit and deny her visitation rights, no problem says the court, you don't' need a reason or evidence to support the your decision; when an attorney says file contempt on her for the dogs, even though it is not in any order, judge signs order to show cause on dogs! When discovery is made at the appellate level of missing orders and file stamped affidavits, more than three hundred pages missing, attorneys stated to the court to place me on supervised visitation, The judge does so without following any course of law at all! It is a self-serving benefit attorneys receive from the courts. The buddy system to get back at your spouse, in the courts!

Another personal benefit courts give to attorneys is child support. For more than ten years I collected child support in the amount of $400 per month from this attorney. Apparently attorneys' don't make much to support children, however are quite capable of paying for a home in full within a four year period and then buying another home paid in full, and three vehicles all in cash. Yet the income is minimal for attorneys and when inquiring about raising child support to his fellow county attorney it was declined due to the limited income. Yet when

Child support for an attorney must be minimal, the buddy system enforces $600 of child support without any income to support such enforcement, even while unemployed, after being displaced from my own home and on supervised visitation, contrary to law. I have received the minimal amount of visitation rights, but who cares, as long as the attorney receives his hefty support money, what matters?

Nothing makes sense or follows law in this case. When emails and phone calls are received from spouses with similar stories, this is not an isolated incident within the Nebraska court system. Many people in the legal profession know how to take advantage of the system to gain excessive favor of the court. The legal scam is well played out, done without hesitation or remorse for filing fictitious documents, false statements of oath and sealing documents with phantom evaluations.

Harassed and denied by the state court system, basically they did whatever their drunken buddy attorney wanted, they bent over backwards to break rules and laws to back an attorney with subjective components of believability. The supposed high standards of the court was continually lowered to accommodate an attorney and his vindictive behaviors.

"Lawyers Are:" Perilous mouths.
-- William Shakespeare

10 SHUTTING THE DOORS ON THE RIGHT TO BE HEARD

Why can the court's comprehend fraud was committed? A court of law cannot be so biased they refuse to rights to a hearing to prove fraud against attorneys?

Integrity of the Bench is very questionable. From the very beginning lawyer-judicial bias was evident, instead of the court applying rules and laws, and listening in a fair and impartial manner, they have acted as an adversarial court based on the anger issues from an alcoholic attorney. Apparently in a dissolution matter you get only one chance, at custody and rights to assets, and when the opposing party sideswipes proceedings at the temporary hearing, through fraud, you are doomed for the rest of your life without rights, the courts crass, defensive attitude of we don't care. I have been completely shut out from the right to be heard from the very beginning. Incidents of alcoholism, fraud and malicious acts by an attorney were completely ignored. Never once did the court ever listen in a fair and impartial manner, never once did they listen regarding rights of hearing from exclusion, never once did they listen regarding the fact that supervised visitation was never enforced by an agency, never once did they listen about issues of alcoholism, and defensive statements that were typical of alcoholism. A system that wouldn't give a pro se the time of day.

The biggest hurdle in the case was not the fact that the court favored an attorney with issues of alcoholism, or his fellow attorney who takes advantage of the system, it is the fact that the right to be heard is extremely difficult because of the automatic bias. Judges favor attorneys. In return, attorneys take advantage of the legal system because they know the narrow mindedness exists, otherwise they would have never played the game. They knew the consequences would be minor in a buddy system. And if the court would have abided by rules and laws, these incidents would have never occurred. It is the favoritism within the system that allowed these attorneys to easily commit fraud, breach ethics and fail to adhere to law and their oath of office. A prejudicial system allows attorneys unsavory injustice to others. It is a system whereby attorneys got away with everything.

When courts fail to follow law of civility, ignore the right to be heard, base orders on deceit and contrary to law, how does one respect law? When attorneys practice fraud, bullying and legal intimidation and are immune from contempt, even at the appellate level? How do you respect law? It's not a fair system, it's a game.

Judges are mean, attorneys are vindictive. The court should be accountable in all aspects of attorney conduct, it is their duty and responsibility to instill a sense of dignity in the court. The court is to live up to the common sense of settling matters in a civil process. The legal system of is one with public rules, rational thought, containing rules of evidence and fact, not a game to be played with people's rights. Ethics, laws and rules are not a "pie in the sky" concept.

The court is accountable to understand and adhere to the rules and laws written by the court. When a person is excluded from home based on vindictive actions, prior to settlement, without due process, contrary to district court rules and law, it is a buddy system. When a person is placed under an order, modified out of jurisdiction, contrary to evidence, finding of fact, contrary to any agency policy or law, it is a buddy system, not a court of law. When a person is continually denied rights of visitation, without any finding of fact, based on vindictive actions by the other parent, it is a buddy system that interferes with parental rights.

When judges are willing to sign any order, contrary to rules and law to benefit an attorney it is a complacent system with vague notions of justice. A court system cannot be negligent in applying rules and laws for some, and ignoring rules and laws for others, especially attorneys. Bias does exist in the court system. It is apparent that the lower court has many ways of protecting fellow attorneys, even ignoring issues of alcoholism. The good ol' boy legal system.

The court does not know how difficult it is for the common person to understand and read the rules of appeal and how attorneys can influence an employee or court reporter within the district court office. Nor does it understand how attorneys behave, with a defiant attitude toward law or rules and the lower court will never reprimand attorneys. Attorneys are misusing the law to unjustly punish without cause or evidence to do so and the courts allowed it. Court itself does not have control over the law or issues pertaining to fact they appear more disinterested in the facts and more interested in the drama.

Thus attorneys have more power and control over the outcome, judges are ready with pen in hand. It is the attorneys who are asked to draft orders and pleadings not the court.

What the court did was unforgiving, placing a huge burden upon my family. There is no evidence to support any of the punitive decisions made in the case, other than pure, simple bigotry. The entire meaning of abiding by rules and laws are so that rights are respected and upheld courts don't victimize families, individuals, women, children, mothers. Court are more interested in protecting attorneys than the law itself.

Yes the courts are accountable, according to the how the case played out, this is a common scheme among attorneys. Orchestrated without hesitation; falsifying affidavits, bait and switch affidavits, and then physically pulling the record from the district court file. Attorneys as such have no problem lying to the appellate court as well, whereby they can make a conclusory statement and improper motion to the appellate court to summary affirm the matter. Even the appellate court is mindset and partial to the motions from attorneys, without the requirement of a brief and Summary Affirmed the matter. Certainly orders and evidence by Supreme Court rules were not adhered to in the lower court, nor does a district court clerk shows concern for missing orders and file stamped, recorded documents. The process if solely based on trust, not a paper trail, or confirmation of documents, following the exact course of law. It's a mean vindictive game, played by the court system and attorneys. Res judicata is not an issue when file stamped orders and evidence acknowledged in the orders become missing from a state file and the appeal court refuses to hear such issues of fraud. Thus an attorney has more privileges and constitutional rights than a mother.

It is obvious that the lower court system that does not follow rules and laws why because attorneys know that it is the Supreme Court that may discipline attorneys. In the case, there was no strict code of conduct, nor does one person have the ability to prove fraud against attorneys. Once a file gets to the appellate level, the higher court gives direction and decisions to the lower court. In the meantime lower courts can run with unbridled arrogance until the higher court informs them of law. Attorneys and court systems, cannot practice in a manner whereby they treat the common citizen as inept, or ignorant of the law. The court serves the people, not the other way around.

A court system should abide by the rules and laws, not engaged in making someone's life a living hell, punishing them without following any course of law. The court got caught up in vindictive actions by an attorney and played right along with them. If any other citizen were to fabricate statements of oath or produce fraudulent documents in court, that person would immediately be thrown in contempt and jailed under statutes, but not an attorney. They receive special privileges of waiting for the higher court to discipline them because judges on the lower court level hesitate to file contempt charges.

Actions by the court system have caused doubt in a public service system. There is distrust in the system, and never would I want to attend another humiliating, lying, punishing court process again, out of fear, another unjust punishment is around the corner. It's a tight knit group, with mean vindictive attorneys and crass, biased judges.

If a person can lose all rights, without following any course of law, a court system that preys upon the ignorance of the citizens knowledge of the legal process, such actions make the Nebraska public court system a GOOD OL' BOY SYSTEM.

A true illustration confirming lawyer-judicial bias in the court system exists even today. A biased system even if the attorney has serious drinking issues it is ignored. By the courts. How some attorneys work the system, as a well mastered scam, as a game to misuse and take advantage of judicial bias. How courts break boundaries of the terms of a dissolution matter to interfere with basic constitutional rights. How judges favor attorneys and will sign an order, contrary to law or rules. How the system protects and ignores issues of alcoholism by attorneys, and above all gives attorneys priority and preference of the right to be heard over and above others, even mothers. And yes, all of these actions by a state court system are infringements of federally protected constitutional and civil rights.

Julie Carper
admin@nebraskaethics.com

"Integrity without knowledge is weak and useless, and knowledge without integrity is dangerous and dreadful."
Samuel Johnson

A SUESS OF
A SYSTEM

If you're not an attorney – we don't listen!

Attorneys have privileges above and beyond
common citizens
    they can lie and deceive,
        it's the win they want to achieve!

Cronyism at it's best!   **Integrity
is a jest!**

Look! Judge Wocket
is in my back pocket
The ex parte order is out of
smorder.

it's not perjury, it's biased mergery!

Proud sponsor of the kick them out give them nothing plan, no need for evidence or need for law, no rules at all!

We like drunken hearsay, and drama, so kick out the mama!

Our standard of decency just happened recently!
We still don't know what it fully means,
 but it's a standard full of beans.

◄IF YOU DONTKNOW THE
LAW NEITHER DO WE

The common citizen is inept,
            That's the way it's kept

Cruel and unusual punishment.... because it's
just a divorce? Some judges have no remorse!

Gee you failed to provide a bill of
exceptions, forget about the deceptions!
Official record is lost, at your cost.

In civil court, it's nothing civil of the sort!
Who would of thought, adversarial form of justice is a plot!

If you think it's going to get better, it's definitely not!

⚡ Nebraska Civil Court Process
If you want to submit evidence you have to go through argument, a court's time not well spent.

The law should be like
a zebra black on white
or white on black,
either way
Nebraska law blends
in as grey, like a jack

Justice is either oblivious or blind to unethical activities in the lower court, they wear thick coke bottle glasses to ignore issues of law, civil rights of parents, and attorney misconduct. Since it is the higher court that disciplines attorneys, attorneys can easily conceal the evidence of wrongdoing in the clerk of the courts office to prevent discovery. The court system is a self-governing, self-serving system. People are fed up with games attorneys play, misuse of law to ruin families; misuse of the legal system to humiliate and intimidate; instead of civility. No court system should show favoritism, over and above the law, especially to attorneys. It is not the true intent of court.

Public trust is lost when a court operates in the capacity of a good ol' boy system. People are not going to walk away from family, life savings, everything they worked for because some attorneys want to play vindictive, unethical games and get away with it, or go through the court system in a long drawn out ordeal. If you can't trust the court system to be fair and impartial, what is the purpose of law or for that fact the court itself?

If we do not maintain justice, justice will not maintain us.
–Francis Bacon

Julie L Carper